T0065536

Come Unto Me

An Outlet for Abused Children

But Jesus called the children to him and said,
"Let the little children come to me... Luke 16:18

MATTIE SHAVERS JOHNSON

authorHOUSE®

AuthorHouse™
1663 Liberty Drive
Bloomington, IN 47403
www.authorhouse.com
Phone: 1 (800) 839-8640

Scripture quotations marked KJV are from the Holy Bible, King James Version (Authorized Version). First published in 1611. Quoted from the KJV Classic Reference Bible, Copyright © 1983 by The Zondervan Corporation.

Published by AuthorHouse 09/19/2016

ISBN: 978-1-5246-3856-6 (sc)
ISBN: 978-1-5246-3855-9 (e)

Print information available on the last page.

Acknowledgement

To Mrs. Audrey Hall, my deepest appreciation for her constant support and some editing, and most of all her abiding love in helping me to complete and bring this book of poems to fruition.

Preface

Come Unto Me

Come Unto Me is also about care and nurturing of children; the responsibility of mother, father and all who bear the responsibility for care of children with guidance, love, patience, hope and dreams. This should come without abuse or abandoning in helping them to reach their highest potential. This kind of introspective caused the author to write these poems.

Lullabies – f rom the cradle to the grave, all of God's creatures find peace, comfort and nurturing in song.

Here the crickets chirping before sundown, the birds before sun up, the cock crowing before day break, the ripples of a stream at evening tide and yes, see the baby as of all creatures falling to sleep with the sound of a mother's voice at bedtime.

It is said that "music soothes the soul!" A sound that all living things understand throughout the universe. The lullabies in this manuscript are just a few of nature's words that can be set to music to lull an infant or child to sleep.

Contents

LULLABIES

If You Can Hear Me

If you can hear me Diana!
If you can hear me, Diana!
Take the hands of my lost
Children.
They are hungry and their
feet are bare
Let them know that
someone loves them
Let them know that
Somebody cares.
Rock them in your arms;
Tenderly and sweet as you
weep.
Take their tears,
softly wipe them away.
Till you are satisfied
there is no fear.
Sing to them your lullabies
Let them cry; bathe their feet,
and let them sleep
till morning comes.

The Papago Children

They pushed them into the desert
Where poppies never grow
Where battles are fought in sand dunes
For food they did not sow

Sprouted fruit from heaven
In the golden parched earth-
Face
Manner served for the reaching;
The prickly flowers of grace

Salvaged beans for winter;
Harvested hope to come,
Summer Flowers of sorrow,
thrust in doors for some.
Footstools of the eagles
a-wait the litol call
while Papago Children's
dried-up tears
build mounds of Cathedral
walls.

Shadows of roots still linger
Behind the scattered few.
Running brooks still flourish,
Beyond the sunset and dew.

Yet in the sun's womb, cactus buds
Produce and quince the
Pangs
Yucca bananas and
Mesquite beans
Control the hunger
fangs.

Come To Sabbath

Come to Sabbath.
Blessings bring,
Children of the Ukraine.
Let them sing
a mountain song,
To the valleys.
Proclaim,
Undying love.
To sunlit flowers,
With drained – out tears
on boughs,
Swinging through
The Clouds.

(Children Who were Destroyed
From: 1933-1945 by Germans)

The Children Of Uganda

The Children of Uganda
Gathered their bodies together
and piled them on their Mother;
A Mountain, silently, begging warmth
From heavens eyes and a
Savior.
The angels hovered over
their sorrow
From years of warfare
and draught,
Watering their tongues from
wells of tears,
and giving needed wisdom
From starvation's cold, cold
fingers.

Children In The Wildness

My Children call from the wildness
They've been there thousands of
years.
They took no bread of redemption
nor advantage of hard work
and tears.

They listen to the voice of Aeolus
Empty but luring their pride
Drawing them deeper in darkness
Leaving themselves locked inside
With crude tools bear to
question,
They hunger for arms stretched
forth.
Their innocent madness keeps
forcing
a search threadbare of worth.

I cannot reach them, tho in
trying
My heart leaps out constantly
asking
What shattered their visage
to cause fleeing;
must they walk in darkness
pleading?

Starving Children

(await Mothers)
Pounding! Pounding! On the kika
open the door, for starving Children
Make the millet-rounds a filler
Dancing on the sands of sin.

Were you there to hear their
message;
To fend the wolves, or act
Chagrin
When they met at baobob
passage
With the love you did not tend?

Dessert games are won
by arrows
Piercing deep the hunter's win,
For you, the path is often
narrow
But whistling winds lay bare
the skin.

An Alcoholic

She had an alcoholic for a mother/father
and couldn't live at
home.
So she cried mountains
of tears
and acted out her
own.

Questions, questions she
wanted to ask
But there were no quick answers
to give
For reasons had been
lost
and no mother there
dared care.

"Pounding on the Kika" by Mattie Shavers Johnson
(Oil on canvas board) 1977

In The Morning Of Your Sun

In the morning of your
sun
Break open the soil of
His trust
Reap his harvest of love as
you must
In the morning of your
Sun
In the morning of your sun
break the bread of life of
forgiveness
The bread of life of trust and love: _
Of faith and obedience;
Your life has just
begun
In the morning of your
sun.

Broken Homes

The fallow of the wheat
lay there
Row by row the stalk
was bare
Fathers run away
Mothers stuck back;
Children disobeyed
From fear and lack.
Mothers kneel to pray
Children, hungry, cry
Enough tears for oceans
to flow by.

What We Need

We need to balance our tears;
Time enough to robe our
fears.
If sunsets guide our way
Though dark as night,
our feet obey.

In The Morning

In the morning we beseech
Your love and faithfully use
your scarlet robe
as we kneel and reach.

Time: It Is A-Calling

The trust within us
will break loose, and free
The promised faith through prayer;
Pass due for our iniquities.

A breath of freshness. O Jehovah!
Praise Him who comes
To break the chain of sorrow
For us, as we borrow
-Hope-
Time, It is a-calling
His vengeance a-waits
To avenge the ocean swell
of pride at sunrise,
To hasten the end done
well.

But without bread
we cannot stay – upon this earth daily;
Our staff, our hope for eternity.
Lord, give us light to show the
way.
Let obstacles fade away
For the night, it is a-coming.

Love Cup

The cup has spilled.
But not my love
It runneth over with many choices,
a drop of freedom;
and screaming voices:

Come fill my cup again!

I cannot "drink to eyes" alone
A greater depth requires;
a fill that quinces velocities
pace;
a burning outside of fire.

The search for beginnings
Increase with time,
as year drink their quantum
and dredges
Left-over levels are not
drawn-down minds,
So we sip, but spill over
our traces and pledges.

Here Comes The Millennium

Here comes a new
millennium
clawing and scratching
its true birth.
Since it's not here;
many, like dice will "roll-
um" and turn
To predict the future
and its worth.

The spoils then will be
tossed inside;
Old friends,
grown-up kinds,
old clothes,
old ideas,
and rides.

Old space-ships for old astronauts
and flowers left outside;
Now glossaries and invention
will take their
place
Beside gas-mask
people grasping for
houses
guns
time
and spaces.

The Family

Family means everything
to you and me;
More than birthdays, Christmas
or Thanksgiving; you see
for it's a bonding of the
spirit, heart and mind;
The power of faith when
forgiven; grudges are left behind

There is a force we
call love
When families come together
and pray
It takes precedence over all
else, of the whole;
Nurturing the value of
the soul;

Reaching up and out for
each other each day
and especially when we
pray.

Family Silhouette Walking Together

The Family

The family is a union
only God can make
Compounded by the whole
with "give and take,"
Proper conception within
while we concentrate,
To determine a peace;
to define our status in space.

The family is a union
only God can make
When you sit at His table
and pray;
Each one contributing
in his own way,
Without fear of reprisal
when issues call for action
of family.
The family is a union
only God can make
He knows each feeling of
rejection
He knows what you
deny

The family is fun, gathering
day after day
No matter the distance
apart
It comes together when
children play
and watches love grow
bonding the heart.

Mama I'm Coming Home To Die
(A Son Gone Astray)

Mama, I'm coming home to die

Don't let'em eat up all

the syrups

Before I get there.

Just give me a quilt

to make a pallet to lie.

I'm coming home to die.

Mama, I'm so hungry

I could cry.

My feet are burning,

My clothes are soaking wet,

My body is dirty; my shirt churning sweat.

I have no learning yet.

I'm coming home to die.

Tell my brothers and

Sisters

To meet me in the heavenly sky,

Tell'em, I'm coming home to die,

Mama!

The Spat

"Give me my toys!"
You broke yours
yesterday
It's on the floor in
pieces
No replacement:
no money to pay."

"Now you've done it!
That is the very end
I'm gonna tell mama!
You are not my friend!"
"I'm gonna tell mama
you took my apple too,
and ate it
That's the second time
You've done this mean
thing to me you've got to quit."

I'll also tell papa."
We need to set things
straight."

The Fallow Of The Wheat

The fallow of the wheat
lay there
Row to row, the stalk
was bare,
Fathers turned away;
Mothers struck back,
Children disobeyed
from fear and lack.
Then, mothers knelt to
pray.
Children hovered, in hunger,
and cried
Enough tears for oceans
to flow by.

The Hand That Rocks The Cradle

The hand that rocks the cradle
is firm, patient, loving and
kind.
It does not falter when
night turns sable,
or wait upon the throng.

Strange is the beauty
Where from she sits;
as a brooder to the nest,
For duty calls, though
Chafe the bit
But all is peacefully blessed.

My Baby's Coming Home

Kill the fatted calf
and bake,
Pies, Chicken, and Ginger Cake
Place the Welcome _____
mat at the door
Clean the curtains
Mop the floor
My baby's coming home.
a lap full of wood-chips
To cook tomorrow' food.

O Mother!

O Mother, did your arms ache?
Did your eyes weep?
Did your heart burn?
Your baby was taken and cast on a ship.
I knew a baby once;
In a straw boat.
I floated with him down the Nile
Hidden among the reeds;
Rescued by love.

Did you feel crushed
like berries under foot
of a giant
Did your heart bleed
like so?
Did you feel a helpless,
longing
Like a vacuum open
and big enough for a tornado to sweep
through?

O Mother, did your arms
ache?
Did your eyes weep?
Your baby was taken and
cast on a ship.

Tobacco And Our Children

Tobacco is "shocked,"
Standing in the fields.
No longer do people ride by; and remark:
"This crop will clear a thousand yield."

They are more concerned
now about
Consequences of smoking;
Cancer is raging among the
lot
Women, children, and men are choking,

From their own habit
They have no one to blame;
Maybe themselves
A "light high" is not work
it
Considering the odds of death
and the pain left.

When Mothers Were Home

There was a time when mothers were home;
Children were nourished and
loved
and seldom took time to roam

They now, take their pop-guns
and rifles
Without feeling; play acting
the scenes
Destroying the enemy in
plain view
But in secret, it is <u>You</u>.

In The Church Where Children Were Burned

In the Church where Children
were burned
People sing hymns and are concerned
When the collection plate is passed
around;
Then Communion is served
in a hushed-sound.

Mothers all on their knees and
pray
Remembering the hate, but their
blessings still say
Their hearts still burn as they
wonder why
Each Sunday morning as time
passes by.

The preacher, preaches a message
of forgiveness;
Ranting and raving the scripture
of peace
There is restlessness as the sisters
shout.
Love will be victorious
when sin is wiped out!

Abused Children

Abused children sit and wait
Their eyes sunken in listless fate
They cannot strike back or call for help
Their bodies bruised in secret kept.

Rage of parents, friends
or foe,
Lost control from previous
neglect as they show
The mind and heart
Separated and ill;
Scars never over-come
emotions never healed.

A chance you take, a chance
you win
To be mother to children
one or ten;
A challenge to learn and
not pretend
you can't fake it, just begin.

Guatamala On The Dump

In Guatamala on the dump
Children live and scratch for
their
food
Day after day; a bag of junk
But to them a fortune is made, though crude.

Their faces distorted;
their skin black,
Lost protein, no doctor care
Searching every pebble kicked
back
along with pigs and buzzards;
their daily fare.

Can we not see or hear
their cries
from across the seas on
waves or title?
Or do we walk blindly
never seeing them die
among the "cast-offs" as
We Walk By?

Made Me A Brush-Broom For The Yard

Worn away, the grass
and sod
Clouds of dust each stroke
its prongs
On to mounds its burning;
its crown

Call to the task of duty
we move
Dancing across the earth
to prove
Our rhythm in time to perfect song
asking approval,
we belong.

morning breaks
the sun –
The flowers have closed
their weary eyes
Sleep baby sleep
Tomorrow will bring
a big surprise
Sleep my baby sleep.

Lullabies

From the cradle to the grave, all of God's creatures find peace, comfort and nurturing in song.

Here the crickets chirping before sundown, the birds before sun up, the cock crowing before day break, the ripples of a stream at evening tide and yes, see the baby as of all creatures falling to sleep with the sound of a mother's voice at bedtime.

It is said that "music soothes the soul!" A sound that all living things understand throughout the universe. The lullabies in this manuscript are just a few of nature's words that can be set to music to lull an infant or child to sleep.

Butterflies

See the butterflies floating
by
They will soon arch the
sky
But will fly away
by and by
See the butterflies floating by.

Baby, Baby

Baby, baby
don't you cry
Listen to this lullaby
Close your eyes and go to sleep
Mama will hold you do not weep

Soft The Wind

Soft the wind blows
through the trees
Soon the sun comes
smiling through
the leaves
W-o-o-o-o-o

Mother, Dear Mother

Mother dear mother,
The comfort of your
arms;
Your voice so soft
and low
Keeps lingering in my
heart so calm _____
I surrender my all to Him and you.

Whenever I'm Sad

Whenever I'm sad,
lonely or low
or not up to par, or weary
facing the foe
You are there _____
To help me weather
the storm through.
You must have been
sent from heaven,
For heaven surely looks
down on me from Him
as I humbly pray.
Thus, His word from
a-far is given pray.
Thus, His word from
a-far is given

Bed-Time

Under cover you must
Sleep.
Now close your eyes
and do not weep
Mama will sing you
a lullaby
I'll see you tomorrow morning
When the dew point meets the sky.

Light Sleepers

Mothers are "light sleepers"
During the night;
They hear every murmur
every cough loud or light.
Just before the early cock
crows
She may be asleep0
But nobody knows.

Before We Sleep

Lets sing a song before
we sleep.
Happy is the one
who keeps
Joy in his heart;
Forever blooming
N'er weeping
E'er growing.

Moment In Space

This moment in space
is a sweet accord
Close your eyes, Hear the
mocking bird sing
Singing love songs while
you sleep
as blossoms and butterflies
Kiss your lips

Close Of Day

The Close of day is very
sweet
Sleep my baby, sleep
Tuck the covers under
your feet
Sleep my baby sleep

Lullabies

I'll fly with you
Little butterfly
over the Hill
up to the sky

While I sing this
lullaby
I'll fly with you
before beddy bye.

!!!!!!!!!!!!!!!!!
!!!!!!!!!!
!!!!!!!!!
!!!!
I'll fly with you
before "beddy bye."

Lullaby

Little one,
Little one,
Please don't cry,
The sun is sinking
Just say goodbye.

It will return with
the morning dew
and I will sing you
a lullaby.

We'll Play: Making Mud Pies

We'll play making mud-pies
Today like yesterday;
Put them in the over on high
And pretend to eat them
Good! We'll say __
Then eat them till we
cry.

Mama Fixes Supper

Mama fixes supper
papa chops the wood,
a lap full of wood-chips
To cook tomorrow' food.

Lullabye

Go to sleep little baby:
Close your pretty eyes
Tomorrow you will
surely rise
And face your dream
and reach for the skies.
Go to sleep little baby
Close your pretty eyes
The road for friend or
stranger, sometimes
Is straight and
narrow
The bush for the robin;
is often sharp with thorns
But always the path of
sorrow
Is chased away with
song.

Cookies And Milk

Cookies and Milk
Cookies and Milk
Milk and Cookies.
Smooth as silk
When evening comes,
We will swiftly eat them.
Nibble and nibble.
Taste and Chew them.

Cookies and milk
Milk and cookies.
Smooth as silk
Soon we'll play
Then sit and nibble them
Nibble them.

Sing Robin

Sing Robin! Sing Robin!
Lift your breast up high
Tomorrow's a-coming
Kiss the promise goodbye.

And the children's laughter
will brighten up the day.
Watch them even often
build their sandcastles at play

Sing Robin! Sing Robin!
Lift your breast up high
Tomorrow's a-coming
Kiss the promise good-bye.

Tucked in Bed - For: Phillip M.

In Mothers Arms

I lay me down
As the grass upon the
ground
Cuddled to each fiber
blade – from birth
nourished from her breast
come down.

She holds me in vibration's
joy;
Singing lullabies on waves of
sound
and sleep comes fast; each
eyelid sunk by
Sundown, twilight, and the
door is night bound.

Grown Up

Hang your clothing
on your hook
Place your shoes by the bed
Read a good book
or hum a beautiful tune
after prayers and said,
Lights out
Sleep tight – croon.

See You Tomorrow
Don' be afraid.

Fairies

Fairies are dancing, my child
with your starry eyes
night is crowned
With star studded fire flies
So to sleep my
baby, bye-bye.

O Mother!

O Mother, did your arms ache?
Did your eyes weep?
Did your heart burn?
Your baby was taken and cast on a ship.
I knew a baby once; In a straw boat.
I floated with him down the Nile
Hidden among the reeds;
Rescued by Love.

Did you feel crushed
like berries under foot
of a giant
Did your heart bleed
like so?
Did you feel a helpless,
longing
Like a vacuum open
and big enough for a tornado to sweep
through?

O Mother did your arms ache?
Did your eyes weep?
Your baby was taken and
cast on a ship.

"Give me a nigh-light
for my room
I see shadows on the wall.
Open the door that I
might call
You can come running
to rescue me, soon,"

"Buy me a flashlight
But stand by the door
I can't go to sleep
without your voice
soft and low,"
"Give me a cookie
and some apple juice,
Read me a story
about the little puppy turned loose
but never me with
Mother goose.

My eyes are so heavy
I can't keep them open
"Just count the sheep, son,
slowly
and ride the clouds
quietly"
Good night!
"I love you."

Printed in the United States
By Bookmasters